Rebirth Of A Flower

Arti Saxena

BookLeaf
Publishing

Presentation by *BookLeaf Publishing*

Web: www.bookleafpub.com

E-mail: info@bookleafpub.com

ISBN: 9789395969147

First edition 2022

to Maitreyi & Atharv

ACKNOWLEDGEMENT

To all the readers who attempted to cherish the beauty of these symbolic flowers. You are the best judge of my lines. Anyone who is aware of their world would be able to relate to these ideas.

I would like to acknowledge the time spent on me by all the people that gave birth to these ideas. This book would not have been written if I had not experienced such emotions.

I cannot forget the efforts of my family who peer reviewed my work and always encouraged me.

PREFACE

In this third trimester of the pregnancy phase, I wrote this book while sitting on the patio of my house and while getting up late in the middle of the night. For the last few years, I have been longing to write a book expressing my thoughts and displaying my side of the world. I tried to showcase my thoughts with only a little experience in writing poems. Using easy-to-understand vocabulary, I have created this version for young readers who get a rush of mixed feelings and emotions. The poems talk about strength, beauty, trust, jealousy, and many more themes. My approach of using couplets in the verses is catchy yet meaningful.

Agapanthus

Love was just a word until you arrived

It meant nothing until you innocently smiled

You cared, caressed and cried

And sometimes arrogantly replied.

But the endless compassion never ended

As your blood was not rented

And perhaps was a gift inherited

To blossom with the blues curetted,

You bestowed the power to tackle the odds

With the shine in your eyes and no frauds.

Though that energy takes all of my time

There is no one that is so prime

To a mother is a child

Who will always be by your side.

Amaranthus

It is not old, it is not stale, which makes me attached

To all those deep connections we hatched.

It is unfading affection, pure and eternal

As a trust of nut around a soul of kernel.

Together we make things easy and smooth

On the road full of rock and ruth.

The intense emotions you take me through

Leads me to nowhere but you.

I hope this does not end anytime soon

Perhaps let me know to pause this tune

But never get faded from my sight

As I am powerless to say anything right.

So, I prefer to be patient and tight;

Keeping our covert relationship upright.

Amaryllis

5

Let the beauty within you shine

Let the wings of pride go loose

Sparkle and give some sign

That makes people confuse.

Transformation is for real

Reflected both inside and outside

Making lives surreal

And thoughts coincide.

You are ready to take risks

While building relationships

Try and do not worry

About being in a hurry.

You are your own judge

Make it right with no grudge

Just be your own cover,

Others will recover.

Anemone

It feels humiliating when I fail,

It feels frustrating when I cannot sail

The ship of desire and hope

With no power to cope.

The part in me that was confident,

Now just needs to vent

The feeling of fading wishes

And fare the well with goodbye kisses.

I have learned to let things go

It is for the better, I suppose so.

Let the mast of luck propel my ship

That might anchor me to the right tip

With no hopes whatsoever

Not now, but sometime later.

Aspen

Hiding under the pillow?

But to the world, you still owe

Your piece of pie

That no one else could supply.

There is fear of losing,

You might be always refusing.

But once given a try

You will, then, want to fly.

Come out of the oven

You are already a baked bun.

Let your cloud of thoughts expand,

Get over it and command.

Don't let anxiety control you

You have the power to glue

The scattered puzzle together

Get loose from that sloth tether

Take your time but get on track

Then there will be no turning back.

Astilbe

In the middle of the night

While looking at the moonlight,

I will keep my book of heart open

For you to complete the words unspoken.

So dear, I will be waiting for you

To reveal to me a world new.

Your presence gives me wings to fly

Not intoxicated but still so high

You give a spark that ignites

My inner concealed lights

That gives me power

To say the things I desire.

I know that you are far

But not as much as like a star.

So, I will wait for you

To share something false or true

Show me the glowing version of my own

I know, I cannot do it all alone.

Bird of Paradise

Fly like you have wings,

Jump so the world swings.

There is magic in confidence

Earn the gift of independence

Roam around the street

Like tomorrow you won't have feet

Explore the unexpected

To get lost in the neglected.

Open your heart

And fall into this art

Of disappearing from the known

Where nobody could con.

A free spirited soul

With no tantrum or troll

Just keep going,

Your soul is navigating,

Your mind is your compass

And you are the Columbus.

Cosmos

Nothing is perfect or crystal clear

Everything is lined by a fine veneer

Hiding a few things unwanted

Making our lives and thoughts daunted.

Don't try too hard

To become the ace of card

Just find the key for a balance,

To unlock the path to a positive valence.

You can't achieve all the world

You are human born to fix the blurred.

Walk away from the bizarre

And make a levelled bar

That keeps you in structure,

Caring for 'what matters the most' juncture

So, take the road you like

There's no other way right.

Cyclamen

Hand in hand yesterday,

Walking apart today

Sweet talks last night,

Today, out of sight

What happened in just one sunrise?

I consoled myself that it was wise

At least we shared moments

Alas! they were not permanent.

Seeing you make new memories

Brings a lot of queries

What was wrong in us?

Why did you make us a hush?

But I suppose you did the right

Then what is the reason to fight?

Still want to go back to that time

When our sweetness was prime.

Laughter, love and hugs

Were our sober drugs.

I cherish that tenderness a lot

Hope you also have not forgot.

Dahlia

I did so much

With no guilt as such,

Went above and beyond

But here is no magic wand.

It was my sincere effort

Which you left in desert.

That is not what I deserve

That is not what I want to preserve.

Treat me with dignity

There is no other complexity.

I can't read your mind

But at least don't be blind,

Don't leave me ignored

Our relationship is not yet soured.

But I don't want to force

Just understand that this is coarse.

Regardless, I respect the things I do,

You don't, so there's nothing that I can do!

Gardenia

No words are ample

To describe you, I'd rather ramble.

The way I take your name in silence

Is loud like playing a thousand violins.

Hope you hear the vibe

I hold for you to describe

My passion and my longing

For an intimate belonging.

I promise it will be quiet as a snowflake

And swift as a snake.

Just play like you own this innocent

Don't stop ! It will be magnificent

Our intensity is incomparable

And our desire is insatiable

So, let's do something weird

Let's get our roadblocks cleared

Just for once make it happen

Are we left with any other option?

Gladiolus

Sincere was my thought

Fears were all fought

Motivation was atop

And confidence didn't stop.

My aims were crystal clear

With the belief that success is near.

But Lord had not planned this way

There were steps that were gray.

I couldn't acknowledge that,

The route to winning is not flat

It is in-fact an iceberg's sharp tip

That led me to fall into a dip

Hiding all the twists beneath

Breaking apart my breathe.

Although my efforts were genuine

The cuts from that tip were left unsewn.

Hyacinth

It's OK to lie

It's OK to cry

It's OK to fight

It's OK not to say the right

But do that all with me

There is no one else to see

The amount of care I seek

Can not be compared with the weak.

I envy those

That share common lows

With you, they express more thought

Than we have things ever sought.

They seem more valued and cared for

While I am left alone to fight my war

Why do I feel ignored?

As if you are getting bored

Of me and our conversations

I hope you get back those sensations.

Lilac

From a seed you grow,

From a stem you flow.

A million signals connect

To make our bond perfect.

You shake me with your moves

Wish there were some cues.

That unseen innocence

Makes my heart caress.

Be assured that you will do great,

The new beginnings await

Our forever love and care,

That we will share

Will be pure and sincere,

As far as we are fair.

The little games that we play

Molds me like a clay

Into a woman so strong

That nothing can go wrong.

Lily of the Valley

The moments that bring joy,

Keep them secured.

Things that annoy,

Don't keep them procured.

Music, art, pottery, dance

Give everything a chance.

These pure forms of art

Is innocent from the start

Gives peace and a sense of belonging

That one has been longing.

Aloof from the fictitious world

But gives a chance to unfold,

A universe of thoughts and creations,

A magic turning hobby into passions.

Just spare some time for this bunch

To give you that punch

Otherwise, there is peace no more

Alas! our busy lives make us sour.

Moonlight

Traveling in the midnight

And wandering aimlessly

Being out of sight,

Drinking booze shamelessly,

Running away from cops

In your four-wheeler box,

Playing hide and seek

So that no one could peek.

It was so random

But nothing so dumb.

There was beauty within

Our actions so twin

Can't forget ever

Will cherish them forever

That magic remodeled us

From rags to riches

Without any fuss.

Even today those actions pitches,

To keep us together

Not heavy on the heart but light as a feather.

Petunia

It is heart-wrenching

To see people entrenching

In evil behaviors.

They are called failures

Who cannot respect one's body

Arrogant attitudes they embody.

Who gave them this right,

To push and grab us that tight?

Stop playing with our freedom,

Stop making us numb

The so-called guardians have no place,

They are society's disgrace.

Their actions are horrendous

Their words offend us.

There is no pity for them

But only condemn.

This rage will not stop

Unless they full stop.

Red Rose

Light up a few candles

Pour in the scent of fresh sandals

A little planning will not go waste

Get something sweet to taste

Cold feet sitting on the floor

Light music is all set to cure

The jitteriness of butterflies in the stomach,

Creating a movie scene to sum up.

Wet hair and that white shirt

Can't stop one to flirt.

The night to remember

Is all set to glow like an ember.

A kiss, a ring and a red rose

Lets you forget the distance and get close.

A little romance can go a long way

It seals the words one had planned to say

Don't know if this is perfect

But seems all correct.

Sea Holly

They praise you unexpectedly

And care for you unconditionally.

They are not your soulmates

Yet perfectly blend in as fates.

No demands, no complaints,

Whatsoever no restraints.

Can someone name that connection?

Can it be termed attraction?

Whatever it is, it is satisfying

Only for a few moments but keeps you flying

Into an imaginary world of castles

Where you are the princess and contain no
tassels.

Don't intervene in the uniqueness

By expressing your weakness,

Making things disconnect

And letting your poles deflect.

Just keep this feeling forever

Without any endeavour.

Veronica

You might be surprised

How many times I have disguised,

Just to keep you connected

And avoid getting neglected.

All the nights spent with you

I opened up on things I had no clue.

There is no chance of resent

On the things, you comment.

Even during our longest spike

I was loyal without any strike

It was deep till the core

Your musk allured me to explore

What was more between us

But you made it all a cuss.

You were my biggest strength,

Couldn't take it to a long length.

Still have no clue what went wrong

I guess this is where we belong.

White Tulip

Trusting me is dangerous

Loving me? Be cautious!

I might be deceptive sometimes

No less than a hundred crimes

The intentions are not bad

It's just my heart that slips and goes mad.

Never wanted to hurt you

But never knew

You were so into me,

That forever was your only key

To lock me into your life.

But certainly, I had a knife

To stab your plan.

Heedless of the dangers in that span.

Excuse me for being what I am not

Honestly, I was just trying my shot.

Wanted more from me but not you

Keeping a safe distance was all new

Letting things go was not my thing

So, forgive me! It stings!

We were better when not a thing.